MW01006644

VOCABULARY PICTURED+
SAT & GRE
WORDS

Sudhir Shirwadkar

Copyright © 2013 Sudhir Shirwadkar

Pictures Copyright © 2013 Sudhir Shirwadkar

All rights reserved. This book or any portion thereof may not be reproduced or used in any manner whatsoever without the express written permission of the publisher except for the use of brief quotations in a book review.

Printed in the United States of America

First Printing, 2013

Some of the definitions that appear in this book are from WordNet.

WordNet License

WordNet 3.0 Copyright 2006 by Princeton University. All rights reserved. THIS SOFTWARE AND DATABASE IS PROVIDED "AS IS" AND PRINCETON UNIVERSITY MAKES NO REPRESENTATIONS OR WARRANTIES, EXPRESS OR IMPLIED. BY WAY OF EXAMPLE, BUT NOT LIMITATION, PRINCETON UNIVERSITY MAKES NO REPRESENTATIONS OR WARRANTIES OF MERCHANT- ABILITY OR FITNESS FOR ANY PARTICULAR PURPOSE OR THAT THE USE OF THE LICENSED SOFTWARE, DATABASE OR DOCUMENTATION WILL NOT INFRINGE ANY THIRD PARTY PATENTS, COPYRIGHTS, TRADEMARKS OR OTHER RIGHTS. The name of Princeton University or Princeton may not be used in advertising or publicity pertaining to distribution of the software and/or database. Title to copyright in this software, database and any associated documentation shall at all times remain with Princeton University and LICENSEE agrees to preserve same.

Acknowledgments

I could not have written this book without the talented artist Abhishek. Thank you for working so hard to make the drawings that appear in these pages.

Thank you to Molly Slavin for her work on editing the book.

A big thank you to my wife Deepa and my two smart young daughters Neha and Tanvi who gave invaluable feedback on all the drawings and helped make sure the mnemonics worked.

Table of Contents

Introduction

The importance of having a great vocabulary cannot be stated enough. It helps you understand and appreciate what you read. To those who wish to give exams like the SAT/GRE, it helps you get a high score on the verbal section. An in-depth knowledge of vocabulary and an extensive word bank helps you score highly on critical reading passages (which sometimes test vocabulary within the context of the passage) and on the sentence completion portions of the writing sections in exams like these. Using a strong vocabulary in the essay portion can also help you score more highly.

Who is this book for?
So if you are preparing for the SAT/GRE or any other such competitive exam, or you are simply just interested in improving your vocabulary, then this book is for you.

What does this book do?
It takes some of the hardest words that appear in competitive exams like the SAT and GRE, and for each word
- provides a definition using plain and simple language
- provides a picture that explains this definition and a way to remember the word and its definition
- explains the usage of the word using some sample sentences
- lists some synonyms, antonyms, related/additional words associated with this word

It is a fact that students tend to remember things more clearly when pictures or other visual material are associated with vocabulary. With this in mind, we have worked hard to ensure maximum mnemonic efficiency.

Please note that this book does not give all possible definitions of a word and is not in any way a substitute for a good dictionary. We have only chosen the most commonly used definition(s) for every word to make the process of vocabulary building uncomplicated and enjoyable.

How do I best use this book?

We recommend you follow these steps to get the most out of this book.

1. Read a word and its definition.
2. Examine the picture closely and the sentence just underneath the picture. The picture helps you understand the meaning of the word and also provides a way to remember the word and its meaning.
3. Once the meaning is all understood, study the sample sentences explaining the usage of the word.
4. You may choose to study the "More Words" section right away or come back to it later.

Understanding the picture is the key to remembering a word and its meaning. If later at any time, you know you have seen a word before but can't remember where, there is a good chance you will be able to recall the picture associated with that word. If you remember the picture and the situation, you can work backwards to deduce the meaning of that word. Chances are good you will be able to figure out the meaning of the word based on the picture you pull up in your head.

We hope you enjoy this book.

Happy vocabulary building,

The Vocabulary Pictured+ Team

Key for *More Words*

= indicates synonym
X indicates antonym
∞ indicates a related word
+ indicates additional words

panacea

[n] a cure for all ills or diseases

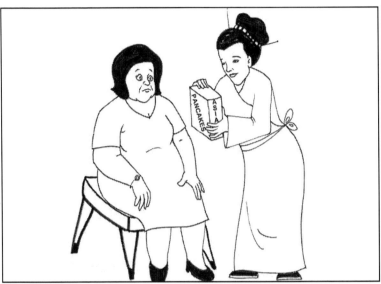

My neighbor believed that the spicy pancakes from Asia were a **panacea** for my weight issues.

More Examples
- The ancient doctor swore that his **panacea** would far surpass all other Western medicine.
- Diane found her home at the beach to be a safe haven from all the stresses and illnesses of everyday life, a virtual **panacea** for the soul.

More Words
= nostrum, catholicon, cure-all

carouse

[v] to engage in a merry party, usually of a drinking nature

Tina got a new car and a new house and she **caroused** all day with her friends and family to celebrate the occasion.

More Examples
- All of the young adults stayed up to **carouse** into the wee hours of the night.
- On New Year's Eve, people often gather and **carouse** until midnight to ring in the New Year.

More Words
= revel, roister
X mourn, grieve

grope
[v] to feel or search about uncertainly or blindly

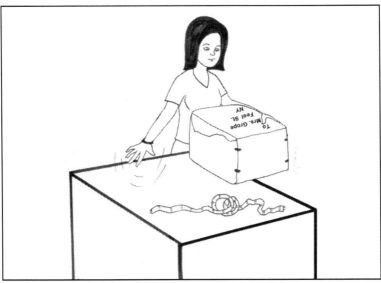

Mary **groped** for the rope with her right hand as she held on to the parcel with the other.

More Examples
- In the dark, Miles **groped** around for his flashlight.
- Ned tried to **grope** through the closet in search for his snow boots.

More Words
= fumble

bedlam

[n] a state of complete confusion

The intersection near the popular bed store was blocked by a lamb this morning, creating **bedlam**.

More Examples

- There was complete **bedlam** when the concert got canceled at the last minute, for people did not know what to do.
- Within a few minutes of the popular actress stepping out of the store, the scene was sheer **bedlam**.

More Words

= chaos, pandemonium, commotion

X order, logic

procrastinate

[v] to put off or delay doing something out of laziness

When Proctor crashed into the net, he wished he had not **procrastinated** on the decision to buy new shoes.

More Examples

- Leigh **procrastinated** until the last minute and had to stay up all night to complete her research paper.
- The weather was beautiful, making it easier for Alice to **procrastinate** and put off the housework for just one more day.

More Words
= dally, defer, postpone
X complete, finish, begin

ostracize

[v] to exclude someone from a group; to shun

To Kim, it almost appeared that the small ostriches had **ostracized** the big ostrich because of its size.

More Examples
- Often teenagers choose to **ostracize** some of their peers for fear of being teased or left out themselves.
- The pack of wolves chose to **ostracize** the weakest one, leaving him behind as they hunted and scavenged for food.

More Words
= shun
X welcome, accept
∞ pariah(n) - a person who is rejected (from society or home)

connive

[v] to cooperate secretly to commit a wrongful act

Connor connived with the customs official to bring in knives into the country.

More Examples

- Baxter was a **conniving** thief who always gave the slip and never got caught.
- Herald and Gwen **connived** a way to obtain the key to the safe, knowing if they could pull the heist off, they would be rich for the rest of their lives.

More Words

= collude

∞ accomplice (n) - a person who works with another in carrying out a wrongful or an illegal plan

enervate

[v] to weaken; to cause to feel drained of strength

The intense heat **enervated** Scott and he had no more energy to wait in the line outside the store

More Examples

- The children's' antics **enervated** the teacher so much she had to call in sick the next day.
- The wicked witch was able to **enervate** all her foes with just the wave of her hands, leaving them helpless before her.

More Words

∞ jaded, fatigued (adj.) – extremely tired
∞ listless, dispirited (adj.) – lack of enthusiasm

fastidious

[adj.] giving excessive attention to detail

Jill was very **fastidious** and made sure that all clothes she delivered to her customers were sparkling clean.

More Examples

- She was **fastidious** in her work, making her one of the most talented and prized artists of her time.
- The clockmaker was quite **fastidious**, able to create miniature clockworks with great detail.

More Words

∞ slovenly – habitually unclean and untidy
∞ exacting – stern, making severe demands

frivolous

[adj.] not serious; trivial

Everybody in the audience assumed that he was a **frivolous** participant when he turned up wearing a frilly shirt to play the viola.

More Examples
- Maria's mother scolded her for spending time on **frivolous** activities instead of concentrating on her studies.
- The group reminded the local leaders of their promise to not waste tax dollars on **frivolous** projects.

More Words
= frivolity (n), levity (n)

sanguine
[adj.] cheerfully confident or optimistic

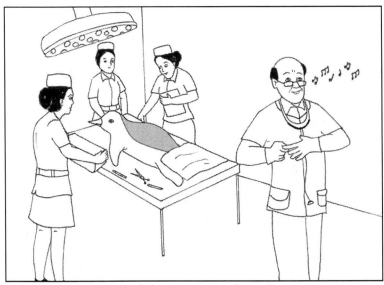

After the successful surgery, the doctor was very **sanguine** about the penguin's recovery.

More Examples
- With **sanguine** pride, Joseph started the first day of his new job.
- Nancy felt **sanguine** as she walked across the stage to claim the diploma she had worked so hard to get.

More Words
= assured, optimistic, buoyant
X pessimistic, cynical

inveigle

[v] to get someone to do something by flattery or clever talk

bagel
in vegas

Tom was able to **inveigle** his girlfriend into lending him some money to gamble in Vegas.

More Examples
- Mandy had always found a way to **inveigle** men, getting exactly what she wanted each time.
- Although it wasn't necessarily honest, Eustace usually **inveigle**d his superiors at the office in order to work his way to the top.

More Words
= wheedle, coax, sweet-talk, palaver

oblivion
[n] the state of being totally forgotten

Crazy Bob slipped into **oblivion** as he failed to adapt his style with changing tastes.

More Examples
- Memories of her father, little by little, passed into **oblivion**.
- Pauli remained in **oblivion** months after the accident, until one day when the coma passed.

More Words
= obscurity, forgetfulness
X awareness

extricate
[v] to untangle or free from difficulty

The rescue team had to cut the trees to **extricate** the helicopter.

More Examples
- I made a point to **extricate** myself from the mess at work before turning in my notice of resignation.
- The laces were in knots and Terrance was unable to **extricate** them from the eyelets no matter how hard he tried.

More Words
= untangle, disencumber
X entangle, embed

nonplussed
[adj.] confused; puzzled

The new teacher had a strange accent and the students were **nonplussed** when she asked them a simple math question.

More Examples
- Harriet was **nonplussed** and couldn't remember where she had placed her keys.
- Marcus had felt **nonplussed** in math classes since he was a young child, and now, in college, he continued to feel lost.

More Words
= baffled, bewildered
X enlightened, understanding

indelible

[adj.] permanent; unable to remove or erase

Mary tried hard to remove the dark ink stains on the floor, but they were **indelible**.

More Examples
- The marks were **indelible**, and so the wall had to be repainted.
- Although they were in a place where no one could see them, Ashley's scars were **indelible** and would stay with her for life.

More Words
= ineffaceable, permanent
X eradicable, temporary

malingerer

[n] someone who tries to avoid work or duty by pretending to be sick or disabled

Jack was convinced that Mike is a **malingerer** as he was often found lingering in the mall on days he had called in sick to work.

More Examples
- Holly was such a **malingerer** and would constantly force others to work harder to pick up her slack.
- Although Janice seemed sick, Gwen knew her to be nothing more than a **malingerer**.

More Words
= skulker, shammer, shirker, idler

prodigal
[adj.] careless with money

Jack was very **prodigal**; he ordered the latest digital camera model though he already had three earlier models which worked just as well.

More Examples
- The **prodigal** son returned home after blowing his entire inheritance.
- Candice was a **prodigal,** and although she made six figures a year, she was unable to keep any of it in savings.

More Words
= profligate
X frugal – living while avoiding waste

junket

[n] trip made by a public official with taxpayer money

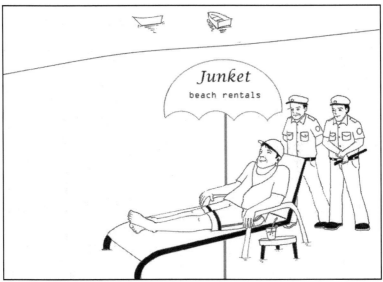

The governor went on a **junket** to Miami.

More Examples

- Mayor Robbie took a quick **junket** to Atlantic City against his advisors' better judgment and without the taxpayers knowing.
- The President of the United States often takes **junkets** on Air Force One.

More Words

∞ malfeasance - wrongful conduct by a public official
∞ jaunt- journey taken for pleasure

serendipity

[v] the act of finding something valuable by chance

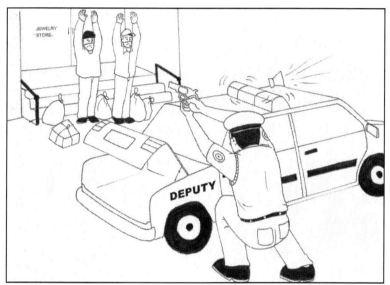

It was the deputy's **serendipity** that led him to capture the two jewelry store robbers just as his car siren was going off.

More Examples

- Their meeting was **serendipitous,** and the two could not believe their luck.
- Wanda knew it was **serendipity** that the home she had always dreamed of was available just when she was ready for a move.

More Words
= karma, kismet, fate
X choice, volition, misfortune

forlorn

[adj.] feeling hopeless

Jack felt extremely **forlorn** after his loan application was rejected by the bank again.

More Examples
- He had been lost for days, and though home was not far, Spot the dog was feeling **forlorn**.
- She was **forlorn** for she did not believe she would ever finish the race.

More Words
= despairing, desolate, inconsolable
X happy, optimistic

impeccable
[adj.] perfect or faultless

Everyone admired the artist's **impeccable** picture of the bird pecking rice on the table.

More Examples
- The wedding was **impeccable,** and everything went off without a hitch.
- Miss America stood **impeccably** graceful before the audience as she accepted her crown and banner.

More Words
= immaculate, faultless, pristine
X slovenly, disheveled, haphazard

ostentatious

[adj.] showy; designed to attract attention

Everyone enjoyed themselves as the **ostentatious** chef served us Austin's tastiest food and wine.

More Examples
- Her **ostentatious** jewelry took away from her natural beauty and figure.
- The Phillips' **ostentatious** home stood out among the rest of the low-key houses in the neighborhood.

More Words
= pretentious, meretricious
X down-to-earth, modest, reserved, plain

obliterate
[v] to destroy completely; to wipe out

The oblong shaped library building was **obliterated** by the huge fire lit by the irate mob.

More Examples

- The hurricane **obliterated** the entire north end of the coast.
- The children were so excited at the birthday party, they **obliterated** the cake.

More Words
= efface, blot out
X construct, build, assemble, erect, develop
+ conflagration - a very intense and uncontrolled fire
+ pyromaniac - a person with a mania for setting things on fire

pittance
[n] a small amount of payment

Phil earned a **pittance** doing street shows with his kittens.

More Examples
- Joyce put a **pittance** towards her outstanding electric bill and hoped they would accept what she could give.
- The camp paid the counselors a **pittance** each summer to stay onsite with the campers, just enough to live on since room and board was included.

More Words
X bounty, splendor, wealth
+ remuneration – wages, earnings
+ lavish – elaborate, wealthy

salubrious
[adj.] healthy

She assured her son that the bean salad was **salubrious** and tasted good too.

More Examples
- She had lived a long, **salubrious** life; perhaps her penchant for exercise was why she lasted until 96.
- With a **salubrious** meal behind them, the two thought a little dessert wouldn't be too bad.

More Words
= salutary
X unhealthy

reprise
[v] to repeat a performance or a musical composition

Jack **reprised** his role of Superman, which had earned him a prize last year.

More Examples
- While the actors were **reprising** the songs, I stepped out of the theater, having heard all of the numbers once before.
- The performers decided not to **reprise** in their final performance unless the audience gave them a standing ovation.

More Words
+ reprisal – an act of retaliation
∞ recapitulate – to summarize, to go over something again
∞ revival – to stir up feelings or stage an event from the past

contrite

[adj.] feeling of regret or guilt for one's sins or offenses

Jack remembered how he had stepped on Connor's hand during the game and was **contrite** when he saw him struggle and unable to write.

More Examples
- Joyce felt **contrite** and regretful after lying to her partner about her past.
- The **contrite** convict stood silent before the court awaiting his judgment.

More Words
= penitent, remorseful, rueful, ruthful
X unremorseful, unrepentant, impenitent

drivel

[n] nonsense talk

Everyone got bored by the drunk driver's **drivel**.

More Examples
- The teacher warned her students to stop with their useless **drivel** and get to work.
- Polly and Wendy stood by and listened to the **drivel** of the cheerleaders as they passed by in the hall.

More Words
= garbage, nonsense, rigmarole, claptrap
X wisdom, sagacity
+ inebriated – drunk, intoxicated

Precise
[adj.] exact; accurate

Tom needed the **precise** size of that smartphone so he could design a skin for it.

More Examples
- It is difficult to predict the **precise** number of people who would be affected by this tragedy.
- Jill wanted to know the **precise** meaning of the word so that she could use it correctly in her speech.

More Words
= specific, stringent, unequivocal, well-defined
X ambiguous, inexact, inaccurate

veracity
[n] truthfulness

The game show hosts claimed that they could determine the **veracity** of contestants' statements.

More Examples
- Emily's **veracity** saved her from losing her job, unlike her lying coworker who was fired on the spot.
- Jenny fell in love with him because of his loyalty and **veracity**, knowing he could always be trusted.

More Words
= verity
X mendacity, dishonesty, deceit
∞ veracious (adj.) – habitually always truthful
∞ verisimilitude - the appearance of truth (Her tanned skin lent verisimilitude to her claim that she was at the beach the whole day.)

scapegoat

[n] someone blamed for the errors of the others

Harry was supposed to look after the goats on the farm, but when they escaped, he made his younger brother the **scapegoat**.

More Examples

- The police strongly denied the charge that the poor suspect was a **scapegoat** and it was a powerful politician who was responsible for the accident.
- He was always made a **scapegoat** for the class's bad behavior.

More Words
= the fall guy

grapple

[v] to cope; to come to terms with

Mary had to **grapple** with the fact that just one apple had grown on the apple tree she had worked so hard to plant last year.

More Examples
- I had to **grapple** with the fact that the news was bad and there was nothing I could do.
- The team had to **grapple** with the loss of their key player to a rival team.

More Words
= cope, contend

acquiesce
[v] to agree a little unwillingly

Rick and Jack's parents finally **acquiesced** to their repeated requests to visit the aquarium.

More Examples
- I **acquiesce** with the rest of the jury that the suspect is not guilty.
- The teacher **acquiesced** to Naomi's request that she receive a passing grade, despite the fact Naomi turned the final assignment in late.

More Words
= assent, concur, consent
X dissent, object, protest, refuse

arcane

[adj.] something secret or mysterious understood only by a few

At the museum, Jack was the only person who really appreciated the **arcane** painting.

More Examples

- The language was so **arcane** that none of the scholars could decipher it.
- Kelly found the society's initiation rules **arcane** and a complete waste of time.

More Words

= abstruse, esoteric, recondite
X straightforward, comprehensible, lucid

mundane
[adj.] everyday; routine; unexciting

After an exciting weekend, it was Monday again, and the thought of going to office to do the same **mundane** tasks made Jim feel like going to sleep.

More Examples
- Every **mundane** morning, Charles gets up, brushes his teeth, dresses, eats a boiled egg, and heads to work at the shop.
- Harriet found school to be quite **mundane**, preferring the open fields at home and her father's workshop where something interesting was always happening.

More Words
= humdrum, ordinary, monotonous, banal
X extraordinary, exciting, uncommon, exceptional

vituperate

[v] to scold using harsh or abusive language

The owner **vituperated** the night operator when she did not answer his phone call.

More Examples
- The teacher had to **vituperate** the class after their poor behavior during the assembly.
- Each week, the pastor stood tall on the altar, speaking of sin as he **vituperated** the congregation.

More Words
= berate, vilify, revile, rail
X praise, commend, extol

ponder
[v] to think over

Mary sat by the pond and **pondered** what she had said that made Tom so mad.

More Examples
- I have **pondered** the question for a while and never come up with an answer.
- Anthony majored in philosophy because he liked to **ponder** the big questions.

More Words
= contemplate, brood, ruminate, reflect

treacherous
[adj.] unpredictable and dangerously unstable

The paramedics arrived and carried Jill away on a stretcher after she met with an accident driving on a road that had become **treacherous** because of an oil spill.

More Examples
- The hikers walk along a **treacherous** path over the snow-covered cliff up the mountain.
- The roads were **treacherous** and flooded from the hurricane's downpour.

More Words
= unreliable, dangerous, perilous, precarious
X safe, secure

inkling

[n] a little hint or suggestion

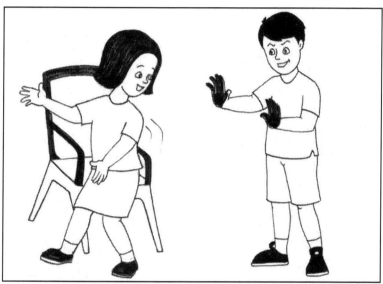

She had an **inkling** about what Tom was going to do to her when he showed her his ink-stained hands.

More Examples
- The pirates wished they had an **inkling** of where the treasure was buried, but without the map, there was no hope.
- I don't have an **inkling** as to where I left my keys.

More Words
= intimation, notion, hunch

imposter

[n] a fake; a person who pretends to be someone else to mislead others

The actress was shocked to see an **imposter** autograph a poster of one of her movies.

More Examples

- Katie was a running **imposter**; she had never run a marathon, and she had fooled her friends and family for years.
- The nice neighborhood doctor turned out to be an **imposter** who had created such a complex backstory and false identification it took the authority years to trace him to the bank robbery.

More Words
= pretender, fake, fraud, sham, charlatan

tycoon

[n] a rich and powerful businessman

The steel **tycoon** and his girlfriend tied the knot on a full moon night.

More Examples

- Although Wallace was a wealthy hotel **tycoon**, he still had a place in his heart for the simple life.
- Kyle came from a **tycoon** family that controlled the local oil company, and as a result he grew up never having to worry about food, work, or money.

More Words
= magnate, baron, mogul

extol

[v] to praise extensively

The Mayor **extolled** the extra benefits of toll roads to the group.

More Examples
- The parishioner of our church **extols** our Savior.
- The king was **extolled** by his people after keeping his country out of the messy war.

More Words
= laud, exalt, glorify
X execrate, criticize, abhor, condemn

futile

[adj.] producing no result or effect; ineffective

The whole exercise of replacing our old tiles with the new ones turned out to be **futile** as the new tiles were just as slippery.

More Examples

- Ivan made a **futile** attempt at his test after he hadn't studied the week before.
- It was **futile** to take the car to the shop, because we knew the engine was shot beyond repair.

More Words
= ineffectual, otiose, unavailing
X fruitful, productive, profitable

desist

[v] to stop

I asked my sister to **desist** from painting on the walls.

More Examples

- The officers called for the criminal to **desist** from running, but he continued to try to escape.
- My parents advised me to **desist** from staying out too late in hopes of keeping me out of trouble.

More Words

= cease

∞ abstain – to voluntarily refrain from doing something

innocuous
[adj.] harmless

The Harmless Inn receptionist assured Mr. Brown that the dog sitting there was **innocuous** and would not hurt him.

More Examples
- The **innocuous** man stood by, viewed as monster because of his scars, though he was kind at heart.
- Although the children played roughly, they were in truth **innocuous**.

More Words
= unobjectionable, inoffensive, mild
X injurious, destructive

gingerly
[adverb] with great care

Jill **gingerly** kept the gingerbread cookies in the oven because she did not want any of them to break.

More Examples
- The artist **gingerly** added the final detail to her masterpiece.
- The new mom **gingerly** held her baby boy for the first time, cradling him close in her arms.

More Words
= cautiously, delicately
X careless, rough

moribund
[adj.] close to death

The **moribund** thief showed his son where he could find more bundles of the $100 bills he had hidden.

More Examples
- The **moribund** dog had lived a long happy life, and was ready to close his eyes for a while.
- The drought had left the wildlife dry, thirsty, and **moribund**.

More Words
∞ stagnant – not growing or changing
+ morbid – suggesting an unhealthy mental state

monologue

[n] a form of drama or a speech in which just one actor speaks

The audience thoroughly enjoyed the popular comedian's **monologue**.

More Examples

- Jack delivered a long **monologue** to the audience while the other cast members were getting ready for the main act.
- To get a job at the theater, Miriam knew she would have to prepare a **monologue.**

More Words

∞ epilogue - a short speech (often in verse) addressed directly to the audience by an actor at the end of a play

∞ prologue – an introductory speech at the start of a play

+ soliloquy – the act of talking to oneself

strident
[adj.] loud and harsh or shrill

STRIDENT ST.

She let out a **strident** cry on seeing the huge dent in her car.

More Examples

- The **strident** scream startled Baxter because it came out of nowhere.
- As they ran through the playground, the children **stridently** exclaimed their joy in playing outside.

More Words
= blatant, clamant, clamorous, vociferous

innuendo

[n] an indirect remark usually of hurtful nature

Jill was not happy with her friend's **innuendo** about her new condo.

More Examples

- Felix was too young to catch the tasteless **innuendos** throughout the movie's witty dialogue.
- Although Samantha seemed to be talking about dinner, her **innuendo** made it clear she was really referencing the recent political situation.

More Words

= insinuation, intimation

∞ allusion – a passing reference or an indirect reference

larceny

[n] to take away something from someone unlawfully

Hint: large sum of money

Robert was arrested and charged with **larceny** after he was caught performing the crime at the bank.

More Examples

- After being charged with **larceny**, the formerly-respected lawyer spent the rest of his life viewed as a common burglar.
- Yolanda could not believe that her own husband had stolen her car and committed **larceny** against his own family.

More Words

= theft, robbery

∞ filch – stealing something of small value

∞ burglary - entering a building unlawfully to steal valuable property

taciturn

[adj.] someone who is habitually reserved and talks little

Stacy, the **taciturn** salesgirl, was of no help when we went to buy a turntable at the local store.

More Examples

- Because she was quite **taciturn**, it took Howard a little longer than he expected to get to know Bethany.
- The elder brother seemed **taciturn** but the younger one seemed to always look for an opportunity to express his views.

More Words

= unforthcoming, reticent, restrained

X voluble, loquacious, talkative, garrulous

+ verbose – using or containing too many words

uxorious

[adj.] excessively fond of or devoted to one's wife

The **uxorious** man gave his wife a foot massage despite being very tired.

More Examples

- Evan was **uxorious** for his love Elizabeth, standing by her side till the end.
- Andrew was nothing **uxorious** to his wife, but accorded her respect and love.

More Words
= adoring
X hateful

diligence

[n] steady and continued effort

He worked long hours daily on his genes research; when it finally yielded results, he was glad his **diligence** had paid off.

More Examples
- With due **diligence**, ants build tunnels and gather food for the colony.
- With **diligence**, anyone can achieve their dreams.

More Words
= assiduous, industrious, persevering, sedulous
X lethargic

enigma

[n] puzzle; riddle; something difficult to understand

Annie couldn't figure out how her grandma could knit so fast; it was quite an **enigma.**

More Examples

- Hardy wondered at the **enigma** before him, trying to figure out how the large boat got into the bottle.
- Mart was unable to solve the **enigma** that was his girlfriend.

More Words
= mystery, riddle, conundrum

jettison

[v] to throw away or toss out from an airplane or ship

No sooner had the boat left the jetty than Mr. Son had to **jettison** the excess cargo to prevent the ship from sinking.

More Examples
- The skipper decided to **jettison** the lifeboat from the ship before it was too late.
- The aircraft was too heavy, so the pilots decided to **jettison** half of the cargo.

More Words
= discard, fling, cast away
X retain, maintain, save

invective

[n] harsh, abusive or insulting language

She covered her son's ears as soon as the TV host started screaming **invectives**.

More Examples
- Miles found her **invectives** to be hurtful and completely unnecessary.
- Kristen was unable to speak kindly to her ex as she typed up one **invective** email after the next.

More Words
= diatribe, vitriol
X compliment, flattery

discern

[v] to be able to tell apart or distinguish

She found it hard to **discern** the expensive marble disc urn from its cheaper version.

More Examples

- Sandra could not **discern** between the twins, although she had met them many times before.
- It was hard to **discern** the road from the snow as Ivan steadily and slowly drove through the snow storm.

More Words
= distinguish, differentiate, determine
X confuse, link, mix up

languish
[v] to become weak and/or fall behind

The tribal lady **languished** in the jail because no one could understand her language.

More Examples
- Ruth **languished** after being sick for over a month; she could barely get out of bed.
- After surfing such large waves all day long, Spencer **languished** on his way home before taking a nap.

More Words
= decay
X flourish, thrive, burgeon, prosper

capricious
[adj.] whimsical; unpredictable

The car salesman explained that the **capricious** nature of the car prices was due to the erratic supply of stock from the manufacturer.

More Examples
- Willard was a **capricious** youth and his parents never knew what to expect from him.
- The dog was **capricious,** and his owners worried he would harm their young children.

More Words
= impulsive, freakish, mercurial, fickle
X constant, stable

condign
[adj.] well deserved; appropriate

Sheila felt that the treatment meted out to Jack at the hotel was **condign,** for Jack knew very well the hotel rules and yet chose to ignore them.

More Examples
- The prosecutor felt that the judges had handed out a **condign** sentence for the criminal.
- The teacher spoke with the principal to find a **condign** punishment for the student who cheated on his test.

More Words
= merited, appropriate
X unjustified, inappropriate

repudiate
[v] to reject as untrue

Mr. Barney strongly **repudiated** the claim that their product, Ray Pudding, caused food poisoning.

More Examples
- The prisoner shocked everyone when he **repudiated** his original story and declared himself guilty.
- When pressed, the daughter **repudiated** her earlier story about how the car got dented and confessed herself to be in the wrong.

More Words
=refute, rebuff, disown
X endorse, accept

skirmish

[n] a minor clash or fight

There was a minor **skirmish** between my boyfriend and his friend when his friend said some nasty remarks about the mesh skirt I was wearing.

More Examples
- Two guys got into a messy **skirmish** before the bartender was able to break it up.
- The teens **skirmished** over who won the race until the coach declared one of them the official winner.

More Words
∞ melee – noisy fight

obsequious

[adj.] obedient or attentive as though a slave

Jill gave an **obsequious** bow to her movie star friend when she asked Jill to get her a new sequin dress.

More Examples

- The **obsequious** servant stood at attention as the lady of the house returned from vacation.
- He was constantly harassed by his **obsequious** employees, each hoping to make it to the top one day.

More Words

= servile, sycophantic

∞ complaisant - showing a cheerful willingness to do favors for others

cavort
[v] to jump, play and dance around with excitement

The pirates started to **cavort** when they found the cave under the fort.

More Examples
- Lee and Amber **cavorted** around the Christmas tree in anticipation of Santa's visit.
- The cats **cavort** and climb among the trees, chasing after squirrels and birds.

More Words
= gambol, frolic, frisk, romp, skylark

umbrage

[n] a feeling of displeasure or offence

She took **umbrage** when I called her dumb.

More Examples

- The **umbrage** hung like a thick fog over the office when the employees realized there would be no holiday bonus this year.
- The townspeople were in **umbrage** after the king conducted an unwarranted raid upon their village.

More Words

= ire, vexation

urchin

[n] a poor and mischievous child

The **urchin** fell off the church steps and hurt his chin.

More Examples

- The **urchin** child had lived on the streets most of her life, and knew not what to do with her new found home at the strict and repressive convent.

- Molly had been spoiled beyond saving, an **urchin** always in trouble.

More Words
= ragamuffin, tatterdemalion

hedonist

[n] a person who seeks only pleasure

Hint: head + mist

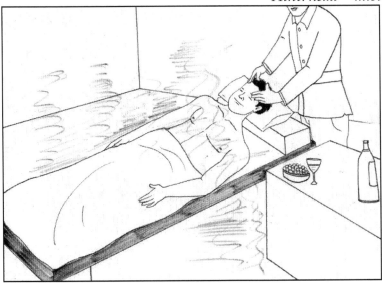

Jack enjoyed getting a head massage, drinking wine, driving luxurious cars and was rightly considered a **hedonist** by those who knew him.

More Examples
- She had lived an ultimately lonely life, a **hedonist** who thought nothing of her future.
- Paula fell in love with a **hedonist** who could bring her immediate pleasure, but nothing more.

More Words
= epicurean
∞ gourmet – a connoisseur of fine food and drink
+ glutton, gourmand - a person who is devoted to eating and drinking to excess

docile

[adj.] easy to handle or manage

Jack wondered if a strong dose of medicine would help make that aggressive crocodile **docile**.

More Examples

- The new puppy was so **docile** that Stephanie knew she had chosen the right one to bring home from the pound.
- Quincy noticed the **docile** children were finally beginning to wake from their naps and were becoming ready to go outside and play.

More Words

= teachable, manageable, passive, submissive, compliant, pliable

X obstinate, stubborn, tenacious, mulish

clandestine
[adj.] secret

Jack had a **clandestine** plan to steal his sister's candy tin while she was sleeping.

More Examples
- Wally took a **clandestine** look into his sister's diary, just to see if there was anything interesting inside.
- The **clandestine** couple hid their love from their parents, just like Romeo and Juliet.

More Words
= surreptitious, undercover, furtive, covert
X aboveboard, forthright

vehement

[adj.] marked by intense feelings or beliefs

He was a **vehement** critic of the plan to build a deli right next to the lake and drove his vehicle into the cement bags to make his point.

More Examples
- Parker feels **vehemently** negatively about the thought of his daughter getting married at such a young age.
- The **vehement** voices of the politicians rang throughout the debate hall.

More Words
= fierce, fervent, ardent, passionate, zealous
X apathetic, dispassionate, indifferent

reminisce

[v] to remember past experiences or events, usually positively

Hint: remember+ mini + scenes

Seeing his little son play with the mini war figurines, the soldier started to **reminisce** about his fond memories with his army buddies.

More Examples

- My mom and her friends love to get together and **reminisce** about their times together in college.
- Sometimes I like to **reminisce** about being young and playing in the woods behind my childhood home.

More Words
= recollect, retrospect

rancor
[n] a feeling of bitter anger and ill-will

As the anchor channel host always spread negative rumors about Sandra, her **rancor** towards him was understandable.

More Examples
- He felt so much **rancor** towards his ex-wife that he hoped to never see her again.
- The **rancor** from the child's mother filled the room with an unbearable tension.

More Words
= bitterness, gall, resentment, antipathy, umbrage
X courtesy, admiration

pillage

[v] to take everything of value from a conquered place

The soldiers **pillaged** the village and left nothing behind.

More Examples

- The pirates **pillaged** the town, leaving no homes standing and nothing behind.
- Children **pillaged** the gifts under the tree on Christmas morning until they were all gone.

More Words

= ransack, plunder, loot, despoil, ravage

abduct

[v] to kidnap; to take away by force

Abby could not scream as the person who **abducted** her put duct tape on her mouth.

More Examples
- The criminals had plans to **abduct** the daughter of the wealthy hotel owner for ransom.
- When Alice and Kyle broke up, Alice snuck into their old home to **abduct** their dog, Spotty.

More Words
= kidnap, hijack, take hostage

ornate
[adj.] heavily decorated

Nate bought an **ornate** necklace for Mary on her birthday.

More Examples
- The Christmas tree was highly **ornate** and stood out from the rest of the more ordinary trees.
- The **ornate** mansion was going to be auctioned next month.

More Words
= embellished, baroque, elaborate, flamboyant, sumptuous
X dowdy, plain

wince

[v] to cringe, as with fear or pain

The prince **winced** when a coconut fell on his head.

More Examples
- Mary **winced** when her mother applied rubbing alcohol on her wound.
- The face the baby was making looked more like a **wince** than a smile.

More Words
= flinch, cringe

inadvertently

[adverb] unknowingly; without intention

He **inadvertently** drew a beard on the girl's face when his attention went to the advertisement behind her.

More Examples

- She **inadvertently** backed her car into the fire hydrant.
- Timothy was surprised to learn that his sister had **inadvertently** lost his keys.

More Words
= unwittingly, involuntarily, accidentally
X consciously, knowingly

dire

[adj.] desperate; urgent

The front tire of my bike was in **dire** need of replacement, even though the rear tire looked fine.

More Examples

- It was **dire** that the message got to the President before it was too late.
- Before the test results we were in **dire** straits and very nervous and emotional.

More Words
= desperate
X trivial

deride

[v] to make fun of; to ridicule

Her friends **derided** her because she was too scared to sit on the ride.

More Examples

- Sometimes children will **deride** others in order to feel better about themselves.
- Although he was a clown, Tim disliked it when the crowds would **deride** him because it made him feel like his career wasn't one worth respecting.

More Words
= ridicule, mock
X compliment, flatter, revere

convalesce

[v] to recover from an illness or shock

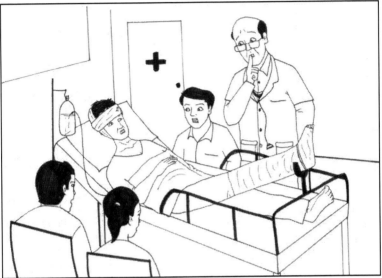

The doctor suggested that we have less conversation with Jack as he was **convalescing** from his injuries.

More Examples

- Not long after arriving at the hospital, the patient began to **convalesce** from the accident.
- Polly could not believe she had been sick for over a month, but at least now she was beginning to **convalesce**.

More Words

= recuperate, recover, recoup

X deteriorate, decline

coincidence

[n] when events happen at the same time by accident but it appears as though they are connected

The three friends flipped coins at the same time and by a strange **coincidence** they all came up as heads.

More Examples

- Paula couldn't believe she ran into Mrs. Edwards just as she was telling her mother how much she missed Mr. Edwards; what a strange **coincidence!**
- Apparently it was not a **coincidence** that I saw my friends at the party store on my birthday, for they were buying me balloons and party favors.

More Words
= concurrent, simultaneous

bedeck

[v] to decorate

Beautiful flowers and big balloons were used to **bedeck** the large wood deck of the beautiful hotel.

More Examples

- May wanted to **bedeck** the new home in a traditional southern style.
- Mom decided to **bedeck** the family room after the renovations.

More Words
= adorn, decorate, embellish, garnish

candid

[adj.] frank; honest and sincere

My friend gave a **candid** opinion about the dance steps I was trying to perform for the grand finale.

More Examples

- The business owner spoke **candidly** about the layoffs that were to come over the next few months.
- Queen Pearl was well loved and lived a long, **candid** life, which made her subjects love her.

More Words
= blunt, frank, sincere, forthright
X deceitful, devious

carcass

[n] dead body of an animal

He saw a **carcass** of a cow on his way to work in the morning.

More Examples

- It stinks in here – must be all the rotting **carcasses.**
- Once Nancy saw the pig **carcass,** she knew she was becoming a vegetarian.

More Words

∞ carrion - the dead and rotting body of an animal
∞ putrefy – to decay with an offensive smell
+ venison – deer meat used as food

recalcitrant

[adj.] resistant to authority or control; not being cooperative

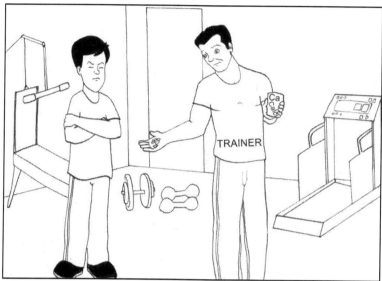

The trainer asked him to take calcium supplements but he remained **recalcitrant**.

More Examples

- As the officer arrested the **recalcitrant** youth, he wondered if it was a difficult home life that had driven the young man to drugs.
- The **recalcitrant** employee refused to follow her supervisor's instruction, resulting in a week suspension with no pay.

More Words
= obstinate, stubborn, obdurate, unyielding, adamant
X compliant, pliable, acquiescent, submissive

maudlin

[adj.] insincerely emotional or foolishly sentimental

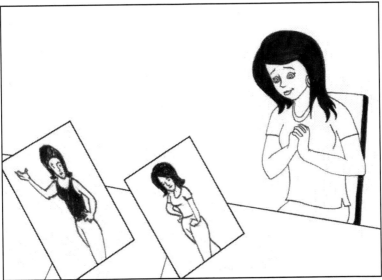

Sarah became **maudlin** and almost started crying after seeing the results of her friend's first modeling photo shoot.

More Examples
- She was extremely **maudlin** at her daughter's graduation.
- The atmosphere was **maudlin** as the congregation sang out in memory of those they had lost.

More Words
= mawkish, schmaltzy
∞ phlegmatic – showing little emotion

travesty

[n] an incorrect or false representation of something

When the judge put the man in jail just because the vest found at the crime scene fitted him, everyone felt that it was a **travesty** of justice.

More Examples

- It was a **travesty** the way the lawyer misrepresented Michael in court.
- Sojourn had been nothing but honest, and it was a **travesty** she had been portrayed as otherwise.

More Words

= mockery, sham

∞ exonerate – to pronounce not guilty of charges

egregious

[adj.] outrageously bad or shocking

Jacks' **egregious** lie made his wife furious and she threw eggs, grapes, juice and everything she could lay her hands on at him.

More Examples
- The **egregious** mess that the tornado left behind was like nothing the small town had ever seen before.
- The guests were quite surprised at her **egregious** use of colorful makeup at such a conservative affair.

More Words
= flagrant, glaring, gross
X minor, slight

transgress

[v] to cross or go beyond a limit or boundary

When she showed up at the office party in a transparent black dress, her colleagues thought she had **transgressed** the limits of decency.

More Examples
- The police chief warned that those who **transgress** the law would be dealt with firmly.
- The children played nicely at the park, knowing they couldn't **transgress** past the sandbox without their parents noticing.

More Words
= trespass, overstep

ameliorate

[v] to improve, make something better

Amy and Leo rated the manuscript highly after the editor **ameliorated** their manuscript with his changes.

More Examples
- Stephanie decided it was time for her to **ameliorate** her deplorable current living situation, so she began looking for a new apartment.
- The medicine would **ameliorate** his pain as soon as it set in.

More Words
= amend, improve
X worsen, degradate, deteriorate

precocious

[adj.] having an exceptional mental aptitude at an early age

Hint: pre-k + quotient

When little Precious promptly found the quotient of 595.55 and 3 and solved other complex problems, the teacher was convinced that she was a **precocious** child.

More Examples
- Already at four, Bobby was **precocious** and excelled in preschool.
- Mr. Sutton found the children to be quite **precocious** and above average in their abilities to play well together.

More Words
∞ prodigious – colossal, huge in size, force or extent (prodigious storm)

solace

[n] comfort in sorrow or disappointment

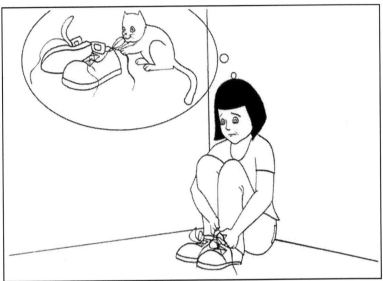

Jill was very sad after she lost her cat and sought **solace** in playing with the shoes and shoe laces her beloved cat had enjoyed playing with.

More Examples
- I tried to provide **solace** to my friend when she lost her puppy, but there was no consoling her.
- Without her family, Abby found no **solace** in her new home.

More Words
= consolation

superfluous

[adj.] more than what is necessary

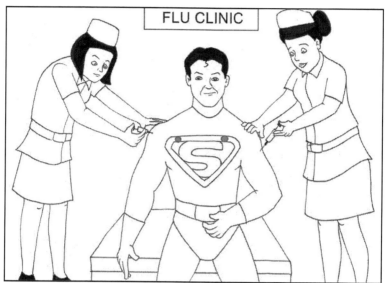

FLU CLINIC

The second dose of the flu vaccine which Superman took might have been **superfluous**, but he wanted to make sure he did not fall sick during the flu season.

More Examples

- The **superfluous** choices at the superstore overwhelmed Candy as she shopped for her husband's birthday gift.
- The mansion held over thirty bedrooms, five kitchens, and a **superfluous** number of lounges, libraries and sitting rooms.

More Words
= redundant, surfeit
∞ plethora - excess

eclectic

[adj.] made up of elements derived from a variety of sources

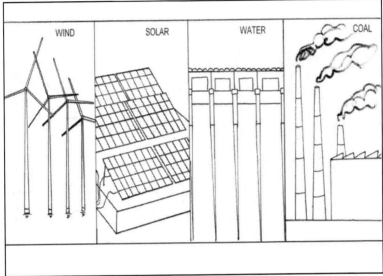

This country gets its electricity from **eclectic** sources of energy.

More Examples
- An **eclectic** bunch of individuals made up the grand touring circus.
- Sassy made it far as a performer with her **eclectic** mix of costume, talent, and personality.

More Words
∞ eclecticist (n) – one who selects according to the eclectic method
∞ diverse – varied, manifold, of different types and forms

incorrigible

[adj.] impossible to correct or improve

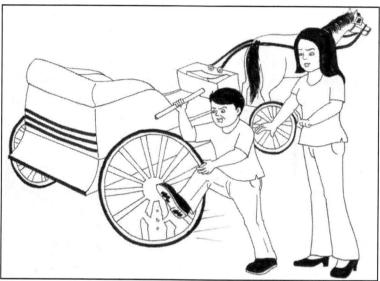

The boy was **incorrigible** as he continued to mess around with the carriage in spite of his mother's repeated warnings.

More Examples
- Betsy was just not able to fix the **incorrigible** & awful painting she had worked on for months.
- The horse was **incorrigible**, a wild beast unwilling to be tamed.

More Words
= irremediable, irreparable, inveterate
∞ irrepressible – impossible to control (irrepressible laughter)
∞ irretrievable – impossible to recover or recoup (irretrievable loss)

defile

[v] to violate the sacredness of; to make impure

She **defiled** the sanctity of the church when she filed her nails inside the sanctuary.

More Examples
- The group of delinquent youths **defiled** the school mascot each year at homecoming.
- Poppy planned to **defile** the facade of the home that had brought him so much pain as a child.

More Words
= descecrate, maculate, adulterate
X purify, hallow, sanctify

fortitude

[n] strength of mind which allows one to face pain or difficult situations with courage

Jack showed great **fortitude** and played an excellent game despite the fact that all of the forty spectators watching the game were rude and booed him the whole time.

More Examples

- With **fortitude**, the brave soldiers marched into battle.
- The king stood strong, **fortitude** on his brow as he faced adversity from his people.

More Words

X pusillanimous(adj.) – fearful

∞ pulchritude – physical beauty

commiserate

[v] to sympathize with; to feel or express sorrow for

The Police Commissioner rushed home to **commiserate** with his wife after learning about her mother's death.

More Examples

- The people stood by during the memorial service to **commiserate** those who had lost loved ones.
- After seeing so many sick patients come and go, Nurse Angie knew how to **commiserate** with the worried and mourning families.

More Words

= sympathize, empathize
+ commensurate – proportionate (salary commensurate with experience)

ephemeral

[adj.] lasting for a short time

The emerald sale lasted for an **ephemeral** period of time as everybody took advantage of the great deals.

More Examples

- Susan soon realized that the joy found in partying was **ephemeral**.
- The **ephemeral** feelings of grief soon passed as soon as Wally's mother scooped him up and kissed his knee where he had fallen.

More Words
= fleeting, transitory, fugacious, temporary, transient
X enduring, permanent

copious

[adj.] in large quantities

He made **copious** copies of the flyers to promote his new company.

More Examples
- The candy store held **copious** amounts of sugary treats.
- Spoiled little Peter had **copious** toys and games and clothes, too much for any one child to ever have.

More Words
= plentiful, bountiful, replete, ample
X dearth, scarce
+ capacious – large in capacity
+ commodious – convenient, large and roomy
+ myriad - countless, infinite, innumerable

trepidation
[n] a feeling of fear

Hint: trap + medication

Randy approached the bottle containing pain killers with **trepidation,** wondering whether he had gotten himself into a medication trap.

More Examples
- Stevie heard the house was haunted, which made him feel **trepidation** as he crossed the threshold.
- It was time for battle, so **trepidation** swept across the front lines, touching each and every soldier.

More Words
= dread, consternation
X contentment, intrepid – dauntless, fearless

sinecure

[n] an office or job that involves minimal duties but receives a good salary

Mark's job was a **sinecure**; all he did every day was sign the material procurement orders that came to his desk.

More Examples

- The captain warned Jack that his job will not be a **sinecure** and he will have to work very hard.
- The position of military battlefield surgeon is no **sinecure**.

raconteur

[n] a great story teller

Barack, our guide on the tour, was a great **raconteur** and entertained us with many entertaining stories.

More Examples

- The **raconteur** often stood by the steps of the church, sharing his stories with anyone who would listen.
- Many great **raconteurs** have come and gone, but some say Shakespeare was the greatest.

More Words
= anecdotist, chronicler

turpitude

[n] shameful, lazy, or unjust behavior

The young men displayed moral **turpitude** when they pushed the lady towards the tar pit.

More Examples

- The man's **turpitude** was unbecoming of him and an embarrassment to the church's established community.
- The CEO had many strikes of **turpitude** against him; he forged a check from the company, used company funds for personal use, and lied to stockholders about quarterly profits.

More Words

= depravity, degeneracy, immorality

∞ iniquity – absence of moral or spiritual values, wickedness

harbinger

[n] a precursor; one that gives an indication of the events that will follow

When Harry won the bingo game, he thought it was a **harbinger** of good luck and that he would soon somehow be able to buy the car and house he always wanted.

More Examples
- The cold winds from the north were a **harbinger** of more snow for our town.
- They hoped that the state of the economy would not be a **harbinger** as to what would come of the housing market.

More Words
= forerunner, premonition, portent, omen, indication

maverick

[n] someone who shows great independence in thought and behavior

Eric was a **maverick**; when asked to come casually dressed for the Friday meeting, his colleagues came in jeans but he chose to wear Hawaiian shorts.

More Examples
- She was a **maverick** in the business world, working her way to the top in no time due to her independent thinking.
- Opie was unlike anyone else in his class, a **maverick** who sought adventure on his own.

More Words
= rebel, non-conformist
X conformist, traditionalist

acrid

[adj.] sharp and strong

Alicia used a room freshener to get relief from the **acrid** smell of the burning rubber outside.

More Examples

- The **acrid** scent of rot and filth lingered down the alleyway where Cody wandered alone.
- The **acrid** desert air beat down on the hikers, tiring them shortly after they began their long trek.

More Words

= pungent, bitter, caustic

X soothing

∞ putrid – decomposed and having a foul smell

∞ rancid – having a bad smell or taste usually due to decomposition of oils and fats

lucrative

[adj.] moneymaking; producing profits

She ran a **lucrative** business designing creative logos for all types of businesses.

More Examples
- Kevin decided to keep all his money in a savings account as these have become very **lucrative** recently.
- She shopped around for a business with an unlimited and **lucrative** income potential.

More Words
= remunerative, profitable
X unprofitable

dolorous
[adj.] tearful; sorrowful

She was **dolorous** after the death of her dog Dollar.

More Examples
- Hailey's **dolorous** feelings lingered long after her cat passed away.
- The **dolorous** music rang through the halls of the funeral home, bringing tears to the mourner's eyes.

More Words
= lachrymose, tearful, doleful, despondent
∞ lugubrious – excessively mournful
∞ melancholy – somber, gloomy in character

nepotism

[n] Favoritism shown to relatives or close friends by those with power or influence as by giving them jobs or promotions

The president was accused of **nepotism** when she made her nephew the new vice president of the company.

More Examples

- Everyone knew the governor was only in office due to the **nepotism** displayed by his powerful brother-in-law.
- While fairly common in the modern corporate environment, **nepotism** is generally bad for productivity because of the influence of favoritism.

More Words

∞ cronyism - favoritism shown to friends and associates especially in political appointments

decrepit

[adj.] worn out or broken down by age or rough use

Because the deck of the house was **decrepit**, Jack ripped it apart.

More Examples

- After many years working in the coal mines, Jimmy grew to be an old, **decrepit,** and lonely man.
- The **decrepit** car could make it no further after it was driven from coast to coast.

More Words
= creaky, derelict, run-down
X strong, able, healthy

idiosyncrasy
[adj.] a type of behavior peculiar to a person

His **idiosyncrasy** was to put lemon slices in a water filled kitchen sink and race them.

More Examples

- One of Will's many **idiosyncrasies** was twisting his hair between two fingers while tapping his foot on the ground.
- Pauli felt Jane's **idiosyncrasy** was endearing and he often laughed to himself joyfully as she would tap her fingers to her chin in deep thought.

More Words
= quirk, eccentricity

canny

[adj.] shrewd and showing self-interest, especially in business

The canny **granny** made sure customers that shopped at her store bought the toys that gave her the most profit.

More Examples

- Amana had a **canny** ability to really make a name for herself in the art world.
- The **canny** businessman made his way with deal after deal, securing both his future and the future of the company.

More Words
= cagey, crafty, clever, shrewd
X inept, naive

braggart

[n] a talkative and boastful person

She acted like a big **braggart** and kept talking about her artwork during the exhibition.

More Examples
- Because Robin often talked about her winnings, she came off as a **braggart** to her friends and family at times.
- Emilia had no interest in dating such a **braggart** as he would not stop talking about himself.

More Words
= blowhard, braggadocio, grandstander, windbag
X introvert
∞ vainglorious - boastful

imbroglio

[n] a complex and confusing problem

Imelda and my brother Leo got caught up in an **imbroglio** over who should maintain the pond in the common area between their houses.

More Examples

- The academic **imbroglio** was impossible to solve, leaving scholars stumped year after year.
- There seems to be no solution to the **imbroglio** in that volatile region as both sides are very inflexible.

More Words
= embroilment

insipid

[adj.] without taste or flavor; bland, boring, or uninteresting

After just one sip, she complained that the coffee was just **insipid**.

More Examples
- The **insipid** pasta lay untouched on the plate.
- The meal was **insipid** and Doug couldn't bear to eat it, so he decided to stop for some fast food on the way home.
- He was an academic who found conversations about popular culture **insipid.**

More Words
= savorless, vapid
X complex, interesting, nuanced, multifarious, multifaceted
∞ lackluster – lacking luster or shine

furtive
[adj.] secretive

The boy gave **furtive** glances at the girl wearing the fur coat.

More Examples

- The detective was a **furtive** person, so hiding undercover came naturally to him.
- She was quite **furtive**, not sharing much of her past or where she came from, which caused a stir among the other townspeople.

More Words
= sneaky, stealthy, surreptitious
X aboveboard, forthright, candid

regale

[v] to entertain with plentiful food or drink

We all **regaled** Gayle with good food and her favorite reggae music.

More Examples
- The servants **regaled** the guests with a five course meal, drinks, and a variety of desserts.
- Grandma and Grandpa enjoy **regaling** buffets at five-star casinos.

More Words
= amuse, divert
X bore, irk

tyro
[adj.] a beginner

The coach asked the young **tyro** to tie a rope around the tree.

More Examples

- She was initially a **tyro** to horseback riding, but took to the sport as if she had been riding for years.
- Although Tom had read all about it, he was still a **tyro** with his HAM radio.

More Words
= neophyte, novice, greenhorn
X expert, specialist, connoisseur

abode

[n] home; residence

"This boat is my **abode**" declared the proud captain.

More Examples
- The doors are always open and the host always welcoming at Grandma's humble **abode**.
- In many undeveloped parts of the world it's not uncommon to find a mix of home styles, from straw huts to tree **abodes**.

More Words
= dwelling, lodging, residence

paparazzi

[n] a freelance photographer who pursues celebrities trying to take candid photographs of them to sell to newspapers or magazines

The **paparazzi** followed the popular actress as she shopped.

More Examples

- The **paparazzi** followed the celebrities as they rushed down the red carpet.
- At this stage in her life, Julia Roberts must be so sick of the **paparazzi.**

More Words

= paparazzo (plural)

regimen

[n] a systematic course of medical treatment, way of life, or diet recommended for therapy

After his surgery Ray was asked to follow a strict exercise **regimen**.

More Examples

- Drew's **regimen** in the military consisted of eating, sleeping, and training for war.
- The camp followed a strict **regimen** that encouraged all the participants to lose weight in a healthy manner.

More Words

= routine, regime

inchoate

[adj.] just beginning to form

In Kuwait, the worker's union was still **inchoate** and a lot of positions remained to be filled.

More Examples
- The **inchoate** chrysalis hung delicately from the tree branch.
- The teenagers gathered together in an **inchoate** group in the hopes of starting a rock band.

More Words
= incipient, tentative, nascent, embryonic
X matured, developed

exacerbate

[v] to make worse

The mother showed the doctor the sorbet her daughter ate that **exacerbated** her stomach pain.

More Examples

- Justine always seemed to **exacerbate** the worst possible situations, making them unbearable.
- Ralph's father always seemed to **exacerbate** the arguments between himself and Ralph's mother, no matter how bad they had already become.

More Words
= aggravate, intensify, magnify
X alleviate, assuage, improve

winsome

[adj.] charming or pleasing

After the little girl won the contest, she gave a **winsome** look to her family.

More Examples

- Henry was a **winsome** young man and had many suitors.
- The small child was so **winsome** that it made Becky think that one day she may want children as well.

More Words
= endearing, engaging
X repulsive, abhorrent

incoherent
[adj.] with no logical or meaningful sense

Hint: ink on hair

Jill was distracted by her customer's **incoherent** talk and unknowingly applied the wrong color ink on her hair.

More Examples

- She spoke **incoherent** drabble immediately after the accident, but with a quick recovery, was able to communicate again.
- The letter was **incoherent** and the general had no idea what the message was meant to say.

More Words
= unintelligible, disjointed, rambling
X articulate, eloquent, coherent

accost

[v] to approach and speak to someone in an aggressive manner

Jack **accosted** the manager of the company when they refused to fix his new A/C.

More Examples

- The officer **accosted** the witnesses at the door in hopes of throwing them off guard.
- Marie thought it best to **accost** her former boss about the way in which she was dismissed from work.

More Words
X evade, elude, avoid, hedge

digress

[v] to wander away from the main topic while writing or speaking

While teaching letter-writing techniques in school yesterday, our teacher said "Let me **digress** here a bit and show you the picture of a tigress I took yesterday at the zoo."

More Examples

- Aunt Bertha tends to **digress** as she recounts stories of her youth.
- I had a professor one who could not get through a lesson without **digressing** from one subject to the next.

More Words
= stray, sidetrack, deviate

castigate

[v] to scold harshly

Seeing his right hand in a cast, Jack's parents **castigated** him for attempting to jump over the school gate.

More Examples
- Grandma **castigated** her grandchildren after realizing they had broken some of her antique dishes.
- The coach felt he had to **castigate** the team after last week's loss against a weak opposition.

More Words
= chastise, objurgate, censure, reprove, rebuke, upbraid
X praise, compliment, endorse

instigate

[v] to provoke; to urge others to take some action, usually of a bad or harmful nature

Standing outside the institute gate, the union leader **instigated** the students to protest against the latest hike in tuition fees.

More Examples
- The school bully tried to **instigate** fights among the other students.
- One of the wrestlers continued to **instigate** the other, hoping for a show down.

More Words
= incite, provoke
X calm, pacify, tranquilize

prevaricate

[v] to lie; to mislead and avoid telling the truth

Jack **prevaricated** when Linda asked him how much he had paid for the racquet, fearing that she would get upset if he reveals the true price.

More Examples
- Andy **prevaricated** his way into a job at a local pharmacy without even going to school.
- The children banded together to **prevaricate** to their parents about how they had broken the bicycle.

More Words
= equivocate, fudge

sycophant

[[adj.] a person who tries to please someone in order to gain a personal advantage

The **sycophant** brought different types of fans to impress his sick manager.

More Examples

- As she met the other students, Cheyenne acted as a **sycophant**, attempting to please the crowd with her compliments.
- The **sycophantic** waiter did everything possible to please the restaurant guests in hopes of a bigger tip.

More Words
= lackey, toady, flatterer

vagabond

[v] a person who moves around aimlessly with no permanent residence

He lived like a **vagabond,** moving aimlessly from one town to another.

More Examples

- After losing his job, home and family, the old man wandered as a **vagabond** for many years before settling down near the sweet shore.
- During the Great Depression, one of the biggest societal issues was homeless **vagabonds.**

More Words
= drifter, floater, vagrant

vacillate

[v] to not be able to decide between different opinions or course of actions

When offered an ice cream, the kid **vacillated** for a few minutes, unable to make up his mind.

More Examples

- She **vacillated** between two different dresses for weeks before finally making a decision.
- Stephaney would **vacillate** for hours before deciding what to make for dinner each day.

More Words
= waver, oscillate
X persist, stay

charlatan

[n] fraud; a person who claims to have special knowledge and skills and cheats customers by selling medicine or other such goods

The **charlatan** promised the kids that wearing the shark charms would help them get good grades in Latin.

More Examples

- The **charlatan** came through the town each year in a caravan and sold to the poor townspeople all of his false medicines.
- So many had trusted Dr. Boggle, just to find out years later he was no more than a **charlatan**.

More Words
= swindler, mountebank, quack

obfuscate

[v] to make something confusing or harder to understand on purpose

When asked how to skate, Peter talked for a long time about the oblong shape of the skates to **obfuscate** the fact that he could not skate.

More Examples
- Drew tried to **obfuscate** the key to the puzzle just to pick on Jenny who already found it difficult.
- There was no need to **obfuscate** the directions, for they were already confusing enough.

More Words
= obscure, muddle
X clarify, elucidate, illuminate

promulgate

[v] to announce

The school **promulgated** strict rules for the prom and displayed them prominently outside the school gate.

More Examples

- Her emcee (*a master of ceremonies*) was to **promulgate** the newly wedded couple at the beginning of their reception.
- At the palace, he was often asked to **promulgate** the royal law.

More Words
= proclaim, publicize
∞ decree, fiat – a legal order

emulate

[v] to attempt to equal or do better by imitating

Mark struck a pose like the emu at the zoo; he always wished he could **emulate** the success of his Olympics marathon gold winner friend.

More Examples
- Tina suggested Jack that he **emulate** his father's strong work ethic in order to be successful.
- Baby mammals in the wild often **emulate** their parents in order to assimilate to the group and learn how to survive.

More Words
∞ mimic, imitate – to copy someone's behavior or looks

impetuous

[adj.] characterized by unnecessary haste and lack of thought or consideration

Hint: pets + us

When Sandra heard about the American doctor who can treat her sick pets, she took an **impetuous** decision to fly to the US.

More Examples

- The **impetuous** teenagers rushed to get married, inconveniencing the entire family.
- Suzy was such a patient person that she often wondered how she ended up married to such an **impetuous** man.

More Words
= impulsive, spontaneous, brash
X careful, deliberative, purposeful

perturbed
[adj.] to be bothered, disturbed, completely confused

The young man was **perturbed** when a cat came purring out from under the turban.

More Examples

- Alexander was **perturbed** at the test questions and wished he had studied harder.
- Ralph was **perturbed**, for he could not remember where he put his keys and he was now locked out of the house.

More Words
= rattled, bewildered, flustered, annoyed
X calm, composed

convivial
[adj.] merry; festive

Jack enjoyed the **convivial** atmosphere and the tasty corn on the cob at his friend's New Year party.

More Examples
- The mood of the entire town was **convivial** as they welcomed their sons and daughters returning from war.
- Logan always found the Macy's Thanksgiving Day Parade to be such a **convivial** event.

More Words
= mirthful, sociable
X antisocial, disagreeable

tranquil

[adj.] calm and peaceful

Hint: train + quail

The atmosphere inside the room where Megan conducted her yoga classes was always **tranquil**.

More Examples
- After a day at the spa, Elizabeth felt quite relaxed and **tranquil**.
- The garden had an air of peace, leaving the passersby **tranquil**.

More Words
= placid, serene, calm
X agitated, chaotic, stressed, frantic

venerable

[adj.] worthy of respect because of age, position, or character

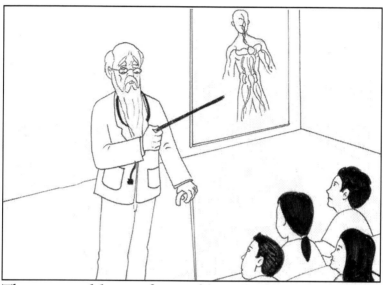

The **venerable** professor likened the veins in the human body to cables.

More Examples

- The **venerable** mentor was aged over a hundred and still wise beyond his years.
- Grandpa was a **venerable** man and made an impact on many loved ones lives through the years.

More Words
= honorable, revered, august
X immature, juvenile, infantile

skeptic

[n] one who constantly doubts or questions

Jessica's trainer was a **skeptic** and always suspected her work ethic.

More Examples

- Norman was unable to keep any lasting relationships because he was such a **skeptic** about the possibility of love.
- The child was already such a **skeptic**, unwilling to believe in even Santa Claus.

More Words
= cynical
X devotee, disciple

dubious

[adj.] doubtful; not convinced

Everyone remained **dubious** about the experiments Dr. Max had conducted to answer the question "Do bees have feelings like us?"

More Examples
- I felt **dubious** about the offer on the house, knowing the price was much higher than it was actually worth.
- She was upset that her husband had hired an interior decorator with a **dubious** track record to work on her dream project.

More Words
= questionable, debatable, ambiguous, equivocal
X convinced, established, trustworthy, unambiguous

abhorrent

[adj.] disgusting; highly offensive; causing great dislike

Alex considered downloading music from the internet an **abhorrent** activity, but his younger brother did not.

More Examples
- Nancy found wrestling to be an **abhorrent** pastime, a mockery of real sports, and a false representation of actual strength.
- Janice found stripping to be an **abhorrent** source of income.

More Words
= detestable, obscene, repugnant, repulsive
X appealing, attractive, alluring

mendicant

[n] beggar, a poor person who lives by begging

The **mendicant** stood outside the store begging for food.

More Examples

- The king disguised himself as a **mendicant** and roamed the streets of his kingdom.
- After losing everything to a gambling habit, Ivan spent the last of his days on the street as a **mendicant**.

More Words

= pauper

∞ destitute, indigent – poor enough to need help from others

∞ impecunious – not having enough money to pay for necessities

chagrin

[adj.] strong feelings of embarrassment

LET'S DANCE
CHA CHA CHA

Alicia was **chagrined** when she fell down doing the cha cha dance and everyone in the audience started grinning.

More Examples
- After falling in the cafeteria in front of all the other students, Debra was **chagrined**.
- The family was **chagrined** at the fact that only a few neighbors showed up to their holiday party.

More Words
= humiliated, mortified, humbled, embarrassed
X proud, confident

preposterous
[adj.] very foolish; nonsensical

They all thought that the tagline of the movie poster was **preposterous**.

More Examples

- Patrick thought the magic show was **preposterous** although his friend believed it to be fantastic and true.
- It was **preposterous** to think he would make it to school on time after oversleeping thirty minutes.

More Words
= absurd, derisory, idiotic, laughable, ludicrous
X believable, credible, plausible, logical

circuitous

[adj.] Taking a lengthy route instead of the straight one

Alex had no choice but to take a **circuitous** route to reach his house as a big tree blocked his usual way.

More Examples

- Getting a chance to ride the four-wheeler for the first time, Sam took a **circuitous** route home to lengthen his trip.
- Terry always seemed to be **circuitous** in completing her tasks at work, unable to get the job done in an efficient or straightforward manner.

More Words
= roundabout, devious, meandering
X straightforward, direct, undeviating, uncomplicated

conjecture
[n] guess

Seeing Jack sleeping during the math lecture, Mary **conjectured** that he must have slept late the previous night.

More Examples
- William made his best **conjecture**, but he still was unable to figure out what was missing.
- Misty knew that even her best **conjecture** would not help and that she would finally have to stop and ask for directions.

More Words
= speculation, hypothesis, surmise, deduction, inference

exasperated

[adj.] very irritated or annoyed; fed up; out of patience

Jack was **exasperated** with his wife's constant partying and shopping and wondered if it was best for them to separate.

More Examples

- Oliver was **exasperated** by all the arguing that had been going on with his roommates and decided it was time for him to find his own place to live.
- No matter how hard they tried, the dance group could not get the routine down, leaving their instructor **exasperated** each day after practice.

More Words
= infuriated, incensed
X patient, unwearied, serene

sabotage

[n] an intentional act of destruction of property or disruption

Tom was angry with his employer and set fire to his boat in an act of **sabotage**.

More Examples
- The soccer team showed poor sportsmanship when they decided to **sabotage** the opposing team's field.
- Alex was a dishonest person who repeatedly **sabotaged** those he worked with in order to succeed himself.

More Words
= subvert, undermine, destabilize, cripple, wreck
X fix, construct

clamber

[v] to climb in an awkward manner, with difficulty

Mike and Randy **clambered** up the rocks to take a look at the clams.

More Examples
- The toddler **clambered** up the steps, eventually making it to the top.
- Frank liked to **clamber** up the ladder and then slide down the slide.

More Words
= scramble, sputter
X to move fluidly or confidently

hospitality

[n] warm and friendly reception and treatment of guests and strangers

The **hospitality** extended to the patients at the county hospital was very impressive.

More Examples

- The owners of the guest house extended the kindest **hospitality** to all of their visitors.
- Daniel thought the **hospitality** department at the resort was well organized and the staff kind and helpful.

More Words

= cordiality, geniality, affability

X inhospitality, rudeness, brusqueness, discourtesy, disrespect

encounter

[n] a meeting with someone that is unplanned, unexpected or brief

I had a chance **encounter** with one my school friends at the grocery store counter.

More Examples
- In the movie, the humans had a brief **encounter** with the aliens before their ship headed back to earth.
- The young man hoped for an **encounter** with the beautiful woman sometime again soon.

More Words
= brush, rendezvous

hurtle

[v] to throw with great force

She **hurtled** the plates in a fit of anger and one of them hurt the turtle.

More Examples
- At track camp, they learned to **hurtle** the shot put.
- She was in such a rush that instead of placing the china carefully on the table, she **hurtled** it to the ground.

More Words
= cast, crash, sling, catapult

nebulous

[adj.] vague; fuzzy; unclear

Hint: no bill

She **nebulously** remembered the restaurant manager saying earlier that he was not going to bill them for the dessert.

More Examples

- The governor came up with **nebulous** projects and requested more money from the federal government.
- Jill had no idea where to start for the science project this year as her teacher had given very **nebulous** guidelines.

More Words

= cloudy, uncertain, vague, imprecise, hazy, unformulated

X clear-cut, straightforward, precise, unambiguous, definite

niggard

[n] a miser or a stingy person

Hint: knee guard

Jack was a rich man but a complete **niggard** who always bought cheap stuff without worrying about quality.

More Examples
- Scrooge was a **niggard** who annually spent Christmas alone.
- Willard hoped as he aged he would not become a **niggard** and too obsessed with money.

More Words
= skinflint, churl, scrooge
X profligate
= parsimonious – excessively frugal and unwilling to spend

Index

38240666R00103

Made in the USA
Lexington, KY
29 December 2014